NUMBER FAMILIES

NUMBER

by Jane Jonas Srivastava

FAMILIES

illustrated by Lois Ehlert

Thomas Y. Crowell   New York

By the Author:

Area
Averages
Computers
Statistics
Weighing & Balancing

Library of Congress Cataloging in Publication Data

Srivastava, Jane Jonas. Number families.
SUMMARY: Explains how every number is part of a
family and functions differently.
1. Numeration—Juvenile literature. [1. Number
systems] I. Ehlert, Lois. II. Title.
QA141.3.S74   513'.5   78-19511
ISBN 0-690-03924-7 lib. bdg.

NUMBER FAMILIES

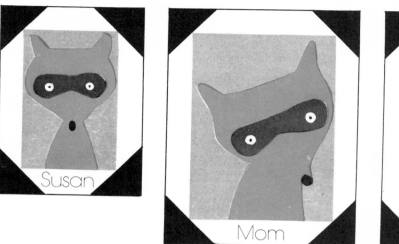

The members of some families are quite a bit alike.

Elsie Grandpa Alice Mom John

The members of some families are very different.

Bill   Uncle Joe   Mom   Sarah

There is always at least one thing that all members of a
family have in common—that's what makes it a family!

1

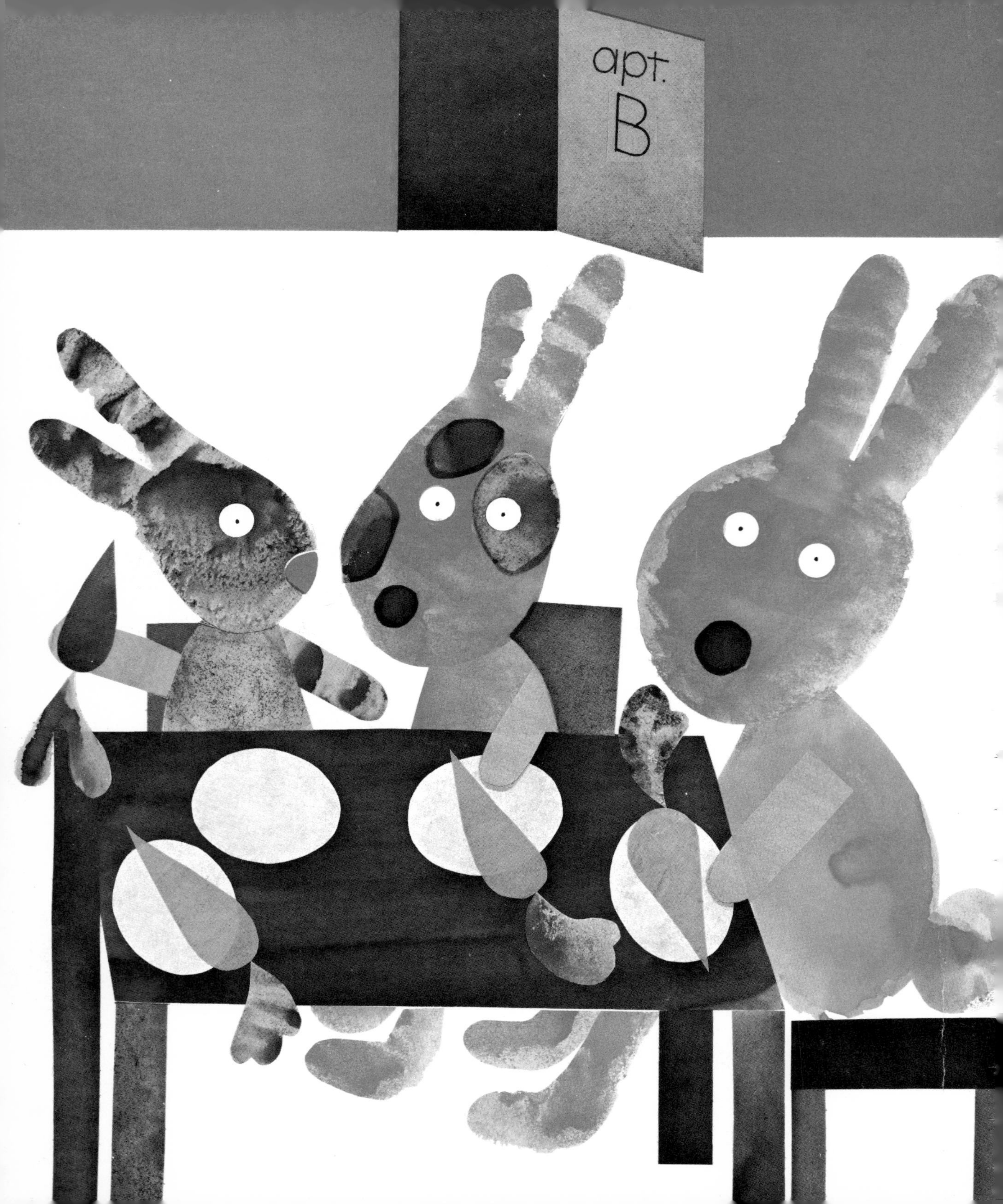
apt.
B

John's family all live in apartment B, 261 Valley Road,
Rivertown, South Dakota.

3

All the members of Bill's family like to go for long walks on Saturday mornings.

Everyone in Susan's family likes to read books.

Numbers have families, too. Each number in a number family has at least one thing in common with all the other members of that family.

Here are some number families:

These numbers can be written using straight lines only.

These numbers can be written using curves only.

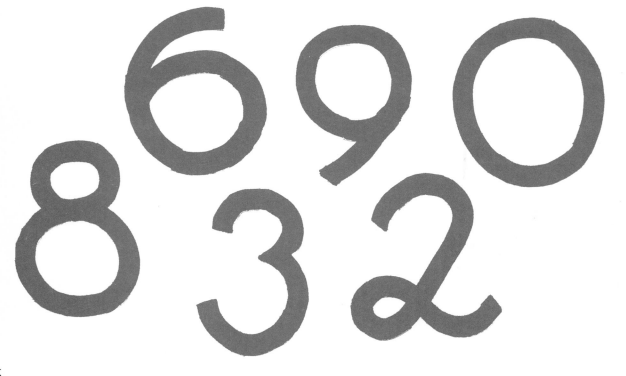

These numbers can be written using both straight lines and curves.

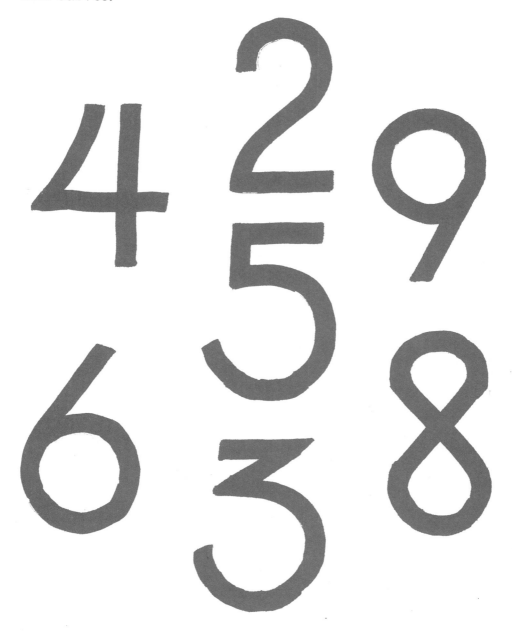

Did you notice that a number can belong to more than one family?

Whenever we talk about 7, we are thinking of this many objects:

Whenever we talk about 11, we are thinking of this many objects:

Get a box of buttons or beans. If you don't have buttons or beans, put something else in a box. You can use any small things which you have lots of, which are easy to pick up and move around, and which won't roll away. Use the objects in your box to find out about number families as you read this book.

11

These are some members of the EVEN family.

20

12

6

10

16

4

8

13

14

Count out 12 of the small objects you have in your box. Perhaps you have buttons in your box. Put the 12 buttons in 2 matching lines like this:

You can always put an even number of objects in matching lines.

Try to put 6 objects in 2 matching lines.

Try to put 14 objects in 2 matching lines.

Try it with some of the other numbers shown on pages 12 and 13.

These are some members of the ODD family.

Count out 9 buttons. Try to put 9 buttons in 2 matching lines.

You will have one button left over. Whenever you try to put an odd number of objects in 2 matching lines, you will always have 1 object left over.

Try to put 7 objects in 2 matching lines. You will have 1 object left over.

Try 13, or any of the other odd numbers shown above.

Which numbers on these pages belong to the EVEN family? Which numbers belong to the ODD family?

20

18

17

9

6

11

14

8

5

If you are not sure which family a number belongs to, take that number of buttons out of your box and try to put the buttons in 2 matching lines. You can list the EVEN and ODD family members you find by making a chart like this on a piece of paper:

EVEN	ODD
8	3
4	7
6	5
14	11
	9

19

These numbers are members of the 2 TIMES family.

18

14

4

20

6

8

16

Each member of the 2 TIMES family tells about 2 times another number. The objects each member of the 2 TIMES family tells about can be put in 2 matching lines with no objects left over. Mathematicians write 2 times 4 like this:

8 ●●●●
   ●●●● 2 x 4

Does the 2 TIMES family have the same members as the EVEN family?

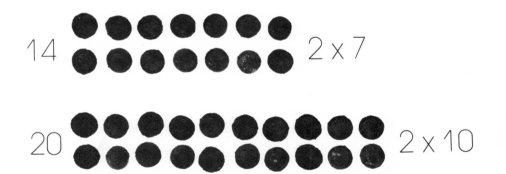

14 ●●●●●●●
    ●●●●●●● 2 x 7

20 ●●●●●●●●●●
    ●●●●●●●●●● 2 x 10

If you are not sure of the answer to this question, look at the bottom of the next page.

These numbers belong to the 3 TIMES family.

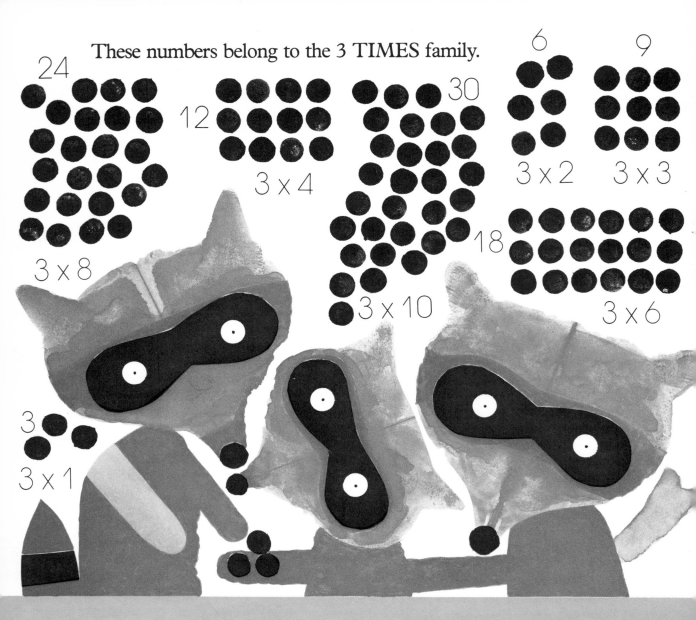

24
12
30
6
9
3 × 4
3 × 2
3 × 3
3 × 8
18
3 × 10
3 × 6
3
3 × 1

Answer to question on page 21:

Yes. The objects that the members of both the EVEN family and the 2 TIMES family tell about can always be put in 2 matching lines. The members of these families have 2 different family names.

Each member of the 3 TIMES family tells about 3 times another number. The objects each member of the 3 TIMES family tells about can be put in 3 matching lines, with no objects left over.

Try to put 15 objects in 3 matching lines.

15   3 x 5

Try 30.

30   3 x 10

Is 21 a member of the 3 TIMES family? Check your answer on the bottom of the next page.

You can find more members of the 3 TIMES family by making 3 matching lines of objects and counting all of the objects you have used.

These numbers belong to the 5 TIMES family.

30

5 x 6

15

5 x 3

25

5 x 5

20

5 x 4

10

5 x 2

5

5 x 1

Answer to question on page 23:
Yes. 21 objects can be put in 3 matching lines. There will be 7 objects in each line.

10 objects can be put in 5 matching lines with 2 objects in each line.

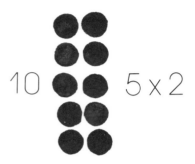

10   5 × 2

30 objects can be put in 5 matching lines with 6 objects in each line.

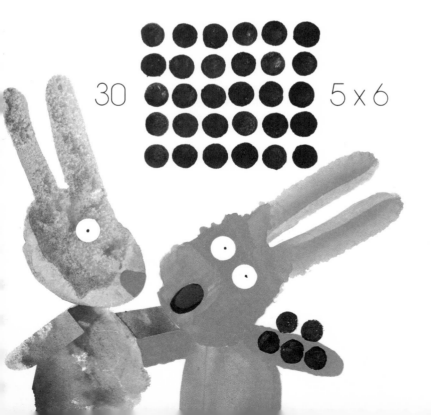

30   5 × 6

25

30 is also a member of the 3 TIMES family.

Can you find another number that belongs to both the 3 TIMES family and the 5 TIMES family?

Try to put 9 objects in 3 matching lines.

Try to put 9 objects in 5 matching lines.

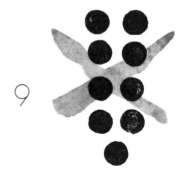

9 is a member of the 3 TIMES family, but it is not a member of the 5 TIMES family.

Try to put 15 objects in 3 matching lines.

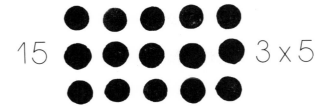

15   3 x 5

Try to put 15 objects in 5 matching lines.

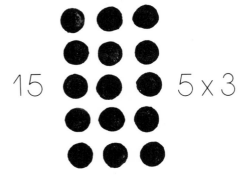

15   5 x 3

You can do it both times! 15 is a member of both the 3 TIMES family and the 5 TIMES family.

Try 45.

Check your answer on the next page.

Every number belongs to the 1 TIMES family. The objects a number tells about can always be put in 1 line.

7 ●●●●●●● 1 x 7

12 ●●●●●●●●●●●● 1 x 12

15 ●●●●●●●●●●●●●●● 1 x 15

11 ●●●●●●●●●●● 1 x 11

3 ●●● 1 x 3

Answer to page 27:
Yes!

45  3 x 15

 5 x 9

Every number also belongs to the TIMES family which begins with its own name. The objects a number tells about can always be put in matching lines with 1 object in each line.

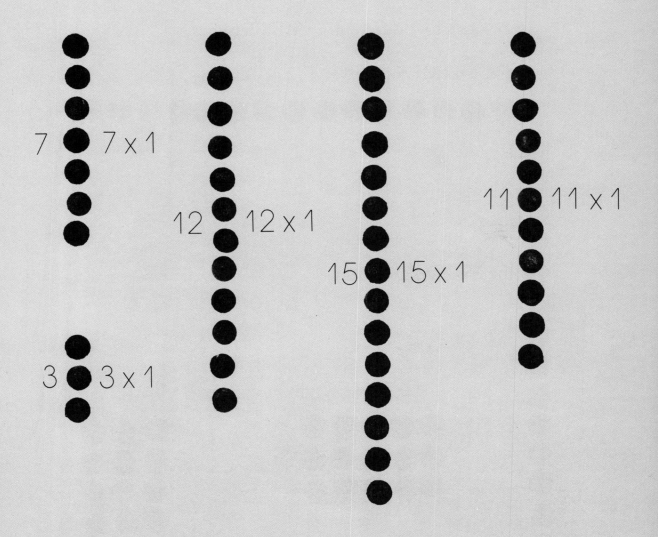

Every number belongs to at least 2 of the TIMES families: the 1 TIMES family and the TIMES family that begins with its own name.

Some numbers belong to many different TIMES families.

15 belongs to 4 different TIMES families:

the 1 TIMES family,

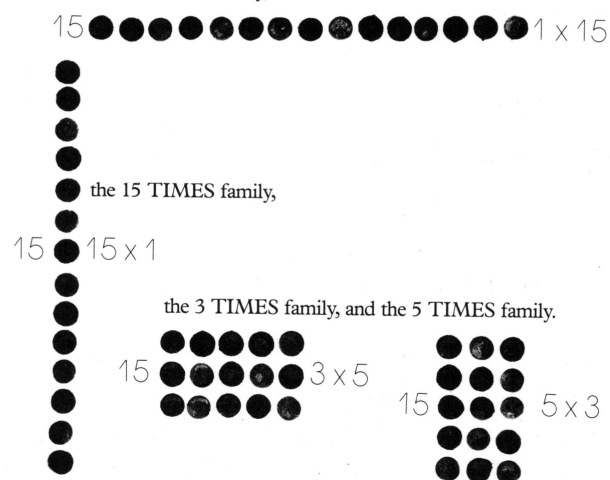

the 15 TIMES family,

the 3 TIMES family, and the 5 TIMES family.

How many different TIMES families does 8 belong to? How many different ways can you put 8 objects in matching lines? Check your answer on the next page.

12 belongs to 6 different TIMES families. Can you find all of them and say their names? Check your answer on the next page.

Some numbers belong to *only* 2 different TIMES families. They are called PRIME numbers.

7 belongs to the 1 TIMES family and the 7 TIMES family. Does it belong to any more TIMES families? Check your answer on page 34.

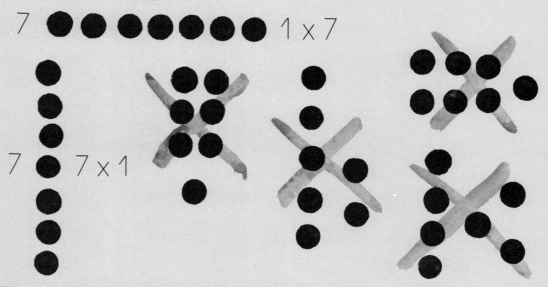

7 ●●●●●●● 1 × 7

7 ● 7 × 1

Check your answer on page 34.

Answers to questions on page 31:

8 belongs to 4 TIMES families: the 1 TIMES family, the 2 TIMES family, the 4 TIMES family, and the 8 TIMES family. Did you find them all?

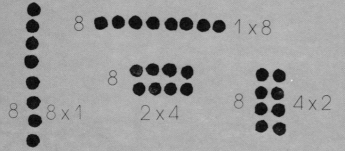

8 ●●●●●●●● 1 × 8

8 8 × 1

8 ●●●● ●●●● 2 × 4

8 ●●● ●●● 4 × 2

12 belongs to 6 TIMES families:

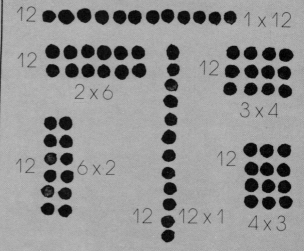

12 ●●●●●●●●●●●● 1 × 12

12 ●●●●●● ●●●●●● 2 × 6

12 ●● ●● ●● ●● ●● ●● 6 × 2

12 ●●●● ●●●● ●●●● 3 × 4

12 12 × 1

12 ●●● ●●● ●●● ●●● 4 × 3

Is 5 a PRIME number?

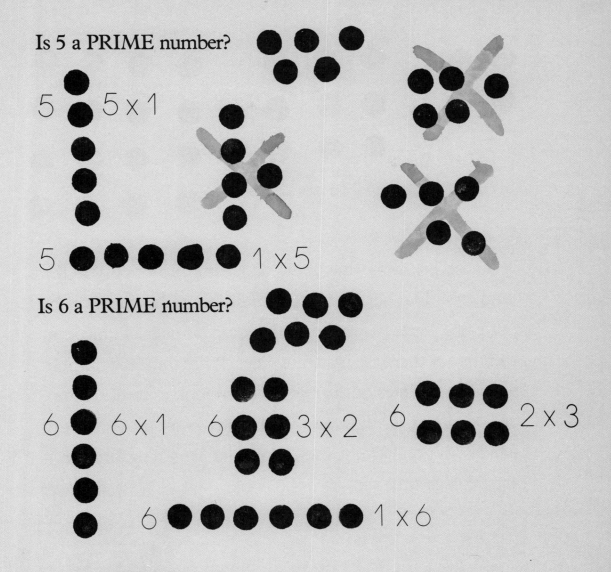

5   5 x 1

5   1 x 5

Is 6 a PRIME number?

6   6 x 1   6   3 x 2   6   2 x 3

6   1 x 6

Is 11 a PRIME number?

Try putting 11 objects in matching lines using 2 objects in each line. Using 3 objects in each line. 4 objects. 5 objects. 6. 7.

Turn the page to check your answers to questions on this page.

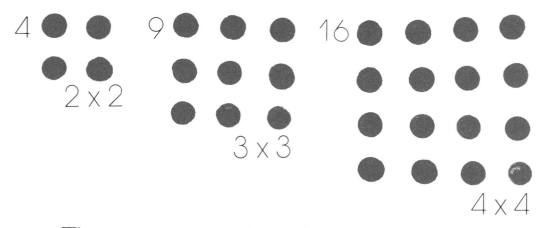

These are some members of the family of SQUARE numbers. The objects a square number tells about can be put in a square. A square has the same number of objects in each line as there are matching lines. It has the same number of matching lines no matter how you look at it: upside up, upside down, or sideways. Turn this book around every which way and count the number of matching lines in a square each time you turn the book.

Answer to question on page 32:
No. 7 is a PRIME number.

Answers to questions on page 33:
Yes. 5 is a PRIME number.
No. 6 is not a PRIME number. It belongs to 4 different TIMES families.
Yes. 11 is a PRIME number.

25

25 is a SQUARE number, too. Can you arrange 25 objects in a square?

Can you find more SQUARE numbers? Check your answers on the next page.

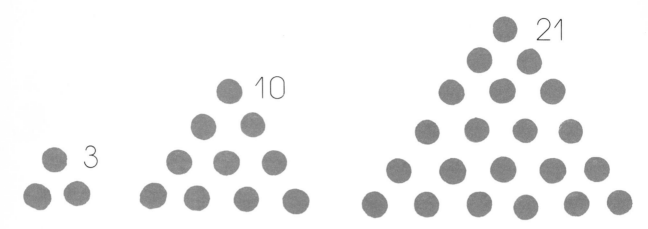

These numbers are TRIANGULAR numbers.

The objects that each of these numbers tells about can be put in the shape of a triangle. Each side of the triangle has the same number of objects. Starting with 1 object in the top line, each line in the triangle has 1 more object than the line above it.

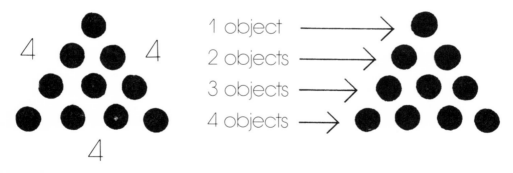

4   4

4

1 object ⟶
2 objects ⟶
3 objects ⟶
4 objects ⟶

Answers to questions on page 35:

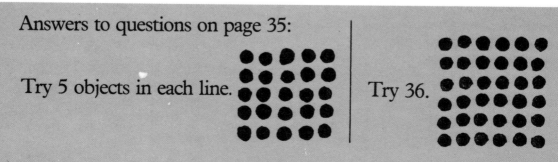

Try 5 objects in each line.

Try 36.

6

16

28

One of these numbers is not a TRIANGULAR number. Perhaps it just came for a visit. Try to put 6 objects in the shape of a triangle.

Try to put 16 objects in the shape of a triangle.

Try to put 28 objects in the shape of a triangle.

Did you find the number that is not a member of the TRIANGULAR family?

Can you find a number that belongs to both the SQUARE family and the TRIANGULAR family?

Check your answers on the next page.

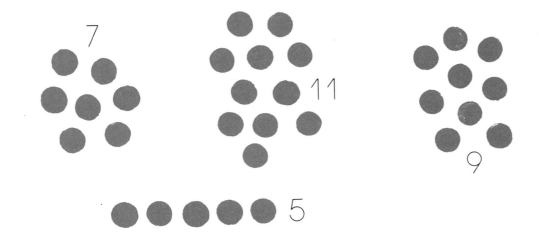

7 11 9

5

Each of these numbers is 1 more than a member of the EVEN family. Do you remember the name of the family these numbers belong to? See pages 16 and 17.

Answers to questions on page 37:

16 is not a TRIANGULAR number.

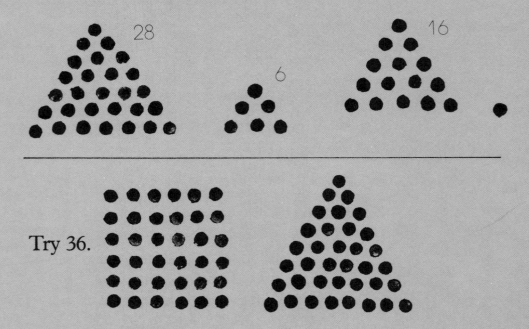

28 6 16

Try 36.

38

12

12

12

12 belongs to the 2 TIMES family, the 3 TIMES family, and the 4 TIMES family. Are there any more numbers that also belong to these 3 families?

Are these PRIME numbers?
Check your answers on the next page.

Answers to questions on page 39:

Try 24.

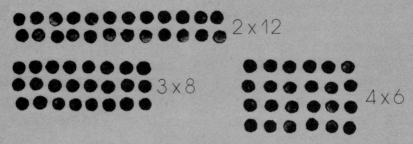

2 x 12

3 x 8

4 x 6

Try 36.

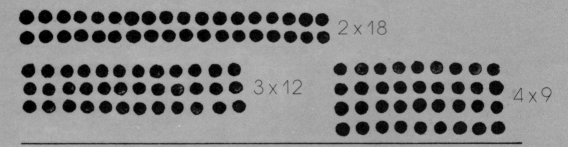

2 x 18

3 x 12

4 x 9

No. If you are not sure why not, see pages 32-33.

Mathematicians like to look for new number families and think about how they fit with other number families.

Can you find some number families and name them?

About the Author

Jane Jonas Srivastava has been an elementary school teacher and has worked on several mathematics curriculum projects. She currently works at home, taking care of her children, Sanjay and Sonia, writing more books, and housekeeping.

Ms. Srivastava graduated from Swarthmore College and received a master's degree in Elementary Education from Harvard University. Her husband is a professor of Biological Sciences at Simon Fraser University. They live in West Vancouver, British Columbia.

About the Illustrator

Lois Ehlert has used animal families to illustrate NUMBER FAMILIES in a lighthearted way. "The artwork is really made of many ink blots, but of course it depends on which blots you keep and which blots you throw in the wastebasket!"

Ms. Ehlert has illustrated many books and has won numerous awards for her illustrations. She has also taught art classes and designed clothes, banners, puppets, toys, and games for children.

Lois Ehlert lives in her native state of Wisconsin.